YOUR SPIRIT MATTERS

GRACIE WARNER

Life Chronicles Publishing
Give your life a voice!

Life Chronicles Publishing
ISBN- 978-0998911465

ISBN-0998911461
Image: Aaqila Thomason
Cover Design:
Life Chronicles Publishing
Life Chronicles Publishing Copyright © 2018
lifechroniclespublishing.com

Dedication

This book is dedicated to my partner, Eddie and my five kids Aaqila, Ayanna, Julia, Kingdom, and Leeann. There were times when I thought I wasn't worthy and you all loved me unconditionally until I loved myself again. Thank you for the support, and I will always love you.

Contents

Acknowledgments

I would like to acknowledge my daughter, Aaqila Thomason for capturing my book cover exactly how I saw it in my mind.

To my mother: Thank you for blessing me, without you this book would not be possible.

Monique Dubose, you were the first person to suggest and support the idea of turning my quotes into a book and for connecting me with my publisher.

A huge thank you to my family and friends: Leonard Roberts, Tina Hightower, Joaquin Thompson, Angela Harp, Gentrie Weaks, Toi Newman, Donnell Gordon, Kecia Glanton, Deshawn Shackleford, Charles Simmons, Melanie Rivers, Rayshon Harris, Micah Diaz and Taressa Brown for their support.

Last but certainly not least, I would like to thank my publisher, Sharon Blake for being patient with me throughout this process. I am a newcomer to the author's world, and she guided me on this journey.

Introduction

I wrote Your Spirit Matters to encourage you to feed your soul daily! Life can become unpredictable, and that is when anxiety, depression, and anger can set in. While reading the positive quotes and affirmations in this book, you can reflect on becoming your higher you. Stay connected to everything good that matters, while attaching yourself to nothing. Use this book as a tool to keep your mind consciously elevated so that your spirit can guide you and help you find your purpose.

Gracie

Your Spirit Matters

Your spirit matters because that's who you truly are.

Your body is just a vehicle for you to have life experiences.

Your spirit lives forever.

You must have purpose in life.

Living without purpose is like getting on a bus not

knowing where it is going.

Find your purpose and know your destination.

Speak love, peace, and prosperity into your life.

If you don't speak it, it will not come to fruition.

Let the Universe know what you want.

It's waiting to hear from you to give you

everything you need to live your best life.

Allow people to grow.

Life is about evolving into your true self.

Don't block someone else from becoming a

butterfly,

just because you want to stay a caterpillar.

Your body is rooted to the earth like a caterpillar.

But your spirit is ready to burst out to live life experiences.

Grow and evolve like a butterfly into the world.

It wants you to grow your spirituality so that you can share your knowledge and use it to enlighten others.

Make an imprint on humanity and wake people up from their slumber.

Loving sometimes means letting go.

Not letting go of the love you have.

Letting go for them to learn, grow, and be happy.

Be it a mate, child, or friend.

You are not here to control life experiences, you

are here to share in them.

So, do what the Universe wants, and that is for

you to be there when needed.

I believe in...

myself

love

having gratitude

being kind

being compassionate

being strong

God.

Stop doing the same "old" thing and expecting

something "new" to happen.

Close the door to endings and open the door to new

endless possibilities.

You are attached to your ego when...

What you do, is who you are.

Your possessions define you.

You care about what others think of you.

Detach from these things and "Find Yourself".

Blaming is what you do when you're not ready to

grow

and learn from the lesson God gave you.

Don't let someone tell you, you can't be happy.

Happiness is a state of mind.

It's on the inside.

It can't be bought or given to you.

True happiness comes with purpose.

When you find it, happiness will be yours.

Through it all God never failed you.

You walked away when you stopped believing.

God is forever.

It's an eternal gift, open to receive him.

Your greatest enemy is you.

Stop self-sabotaging.

You are here to go through trials and tribulations

to show others that if you made it through, they

can too.

Your level of education does not dictate what you

are capable of doing.

God put an inner knowledge in you that just needs

to be tapped into.

You were born to win.

Let God fight your battles.

He wants you to use your mind to create not

destroy.

Don't let the way others see you impact how you see yourself.

Your intentions will show up in your life

so make sure they are in the best interest of you

and others.

Life will sometimes be hard.

Fight back and know that you were given the

strength to do the impossible.

If you want it bad enough, it is worth fighting

for.

Forgiveness doesn't mean you are forgetting what

happened to you.

It means that you have grown to know that not

forgiving is only hurting you and no one else.

There are signs all around trying to guide you.

Just take time to notice them.

When you do the route will become easier.

Don't spend time looking back on the past when
you have so much more to look forward to.
You can't see what's in front of you if you are
always looking back.

You awaken to the light but are still sleeping.

When you awaken to the world you will notice the

light, appreciate it and shine.

You may wonder why you can't get ahead.

It's because you're filled with envy and jealousy.

With that energy nothing will ever come to you.

If you think nobody else is deserving, then why

should you be.

Take life by the horns.

It may jerk you around a little bit but keep

holding on and ride it out.

Don't let anyone put a time limit on your dream.

As long as you continue to believe in it and take

action, it will come to pass.

Only God knows when the time is right.

Don't get upset when the spotlight is not on you.

God may want you to shine without a light.

When you serve sometimes God wants it to be in

silence.

The world is going into a transformation of

awakening your conscious.

You are in control of yourself.

It's time for you to own your truth, whatever it

is.

Give the people that were hurt by you a chance

to heal.

In doing so your healing will also come.

Society may shun you for doing the right thing.

God will put a shine on you for doing the right

thing.

Owning your truth will always prevail.

We are taught to do things for ourselves, and

asking for help is a sign of weakness.

It's really a symbol of strength to know when to

ask for help.

How you treat others is a reflection of yourself.

So be careful of what you are reflecting.

Step outside of your shell to see the spirit in you

that is trying to come alive.

Unleash the power you have been given to be who

you want to be.

Take the first step and God will see you

through.

Become the light the Universe is waiting to see

shine.

It is also alive, and would like to see the beauty

in you, like you see the beauty in it.

Sometimes things happen that are out of your

control.

What you can control is how you react.

Be still and listen to God.

He is always in control and he will give you the

next step.

Take time out to meditate.

Meditating takes you to the spiritual realm where

you connect with your true self.

Your answers are there if you just be still.

Conflict is never a resolution to a problem.

Approach it with understanding.

When you look at it that way, you see it through

clearer eyes.

Your spirit knows which direction you should be

heading.

So, if you are doing something that doesn't feel

right, change direction.

It's your spirit speaking.

You are in control of your own life.

Stop letting people tell you how to live.

Take back control and tell them that you are the

Captain of your ship.

If you are in need of a helping mate, you will

ask.

Life is like a puzzle.

Everything doesn't fit.

Find the pieces that fit you.

Once that happens the puzzle will come together

so you can see the full picture.

You were born with a purpose

Don't walk around like a speck of light.

Shine bright like a star so that others will see

your light and want to shine.

Humanity is waiting on you to illuminate the world

with love, peace, and harmony.

Having gratitude should be a way of life.

It's a way to show the Universe that you are

forever grateful for what it has given you.

The good and even the bad times.

The bad times were lessons to get you back on

track.

So, in everything, always thank him.

You have untapped natural talents and skills inside

of you.

Spend some time with yourself to find out what

they are.

When you discover them, give the world your all

and "tap out".

You are beautiful flowers trying to grow.

Sometimes negative thoughts form like weeds and

try to suffocate you.

Abandon those thoughts for more positive ones.

Disrupt the weeds and blossom.

Treat life like pumping gas.

Pump tenacity, perseverance and patience into

your heart daily.

Fill it up with love and understanding and then

drive out into the world and share all that is in

you.

Never give up on your dreams.

Continue to persevere with intent and action.

Just when you think things are not coming

together and about to have a breakdown.

God will give you a breakthrough.

Life is not about how much you can get out of it.

It's about how much you can give to it.

God put a purpose in you to succeed and serve

humanity.

Find it and give it all you got.

Success was a touch away and then you gave up.

What you failed to realize is that there is always

a storm before the calm.

God wants you to remember you didn't do it alone.

You are always asking of God.

Take the time to focus more on what God wants.

If you seek the things he wants from you, all of

your desires will be met.

A tree stands alone in its power.

It gives us beauty, food, and oxygen.

You too have that same power.

Break your state of mind and believe in yourself.

Surely if God gave that much power to a tree,

Imagine what's on the inside of you.

You are here to shine your light to enlighten

others for them to want to shine also.

So, let your light shine so bright that everyone

will want to be "Lit" like you.

We are here to live the life our higher self

wants us to live.

Each day you wake is a chance for you to start

something new.

Release your fears and anxiety.

Step out and get your feet wet.

There is a vast ocean of possibilities waiting on

you to dive in and grab them.

Stop trying to be the person that everyone else

sees you as and become who you want to be.

You are miserable because you are living a life

that is not yours.

Take control of your life and be your genuine

self.

You are here to please God and he wants you

happy.

Set goals.

Write them down.

Place them where they can be seen daily.

Wake up with intention on doing something to work

towards them every day.

Intent is going to keep you focused to stay the

course.

Like building a house, with each brick laid you

can begin to see the foundation.

Keep building until the house is complete.

When you find purpose, it will feel like you are

on top of the world.

Nobody will be able to stop you from your mission.

The power coming for the inside will exhilarate

you.

From that point on your mind will rise to

ascension.

Stop becoming overwhelmed with problems.

God is here to handle those things for you.

He already has the solutions.

You are blocking the answers with your worrying.

Release your worries to receive the answers God

is trying to give you.

Don't let struggles, shame, resentment, and guilt

stand between you and your vision.

Let go of those feelings.

Write it, speak it, hit something.

Do whatever you have to do to move forward and

have the life you deserve.

Let go of the past.

It is no longer serving you.

Move forward and see what else life has to offer

you.

It's up to you to create what you desire.

You can't do that living in the past.

Live in the present moment and find your purpose.

God has put everything you need inside of you.

Just embrace it.

It is the power.

Access that power.

You will wake up and never sleep again.

A part of getting to know God is standing in your

truth.

When you stand in front of God owning who you

are.

No one else can stand in your way.

Some people are not supportive because they are

in a place where they can't accept the

fact that you have evolved into the person

you wanted to become while they are still

in the same place.

It's hard for them to comprehend that you have

the mind of an eagle ready to soar while

they are still thinking like a chicken

running around in a coop.

Have direction in life.

Without direction you are just cruising around

without a destination.

It's cool if you are just joyriding.

But this is your life, you can only joyride for a

while.

Eventually a destination has to be chosen.

Slow down and start experiencing life.

Everyone is in the fast lane going nowhere fast.

You don't have to be everywhere all of the time.

Take time out to get to know yourself and stop

trying to get noticed.

People will notice you when you do something

recognizable.

Your life is filled with an ocean of possibilities.

Put on your gear, dive in, and figure out which

ones are best for you.

Today is a good time for you to take time to get

to know the "Real" you.

Ask yourself.

What do I really want out of life?

Devise a plan, create, manifest.

The true you is waiting.

Life is like trying to climb to the peak of a
mountain.

There will be obstacles and stumbles on the way.

If you continue to climb you will ultimately get to
the top.

When you get there, you will begin to see a
whole new outlook.

When you have trauma in life, don't let it dwell

into your mind and get stuck.

Allowing it to stick doesn't give you closure.

Your level of maturity is there where the action

took place, being held hostage.

You won't be released until you let go and allow

your mind to heal.

Your attitude not only affect you, but it also

affects others around you.

So, don't walk around sad or angry, showing your

dark side.

Someone may need you to shine your light on

them.

Sometimes when God place people in your life it is

not meant for you to have a lifetime friendship.

God uses people to help and teach us lessons.

Once that lesson is learned, and that help is

given, it's time to move on.

He only wanted that person in your life for those

seasons.

Don't be sad, let go with love and know that God

is changing things for you.

He knows what is best.

Your needs will be provided.

It would be foolish to continue to focus on what

has been given to you.

Vision something greater than food and shelter.

That is menial to the Universe.

Dream a vision without limitations.

I don't care where you are in life.

Dream a great dream.

Go deep inside and find that purpose burning to

break through,

The Universe is waiting on you.

You deserve it.

Stop following behind people.

You have a clear path of success inside of you.

Just wake up and choose the right direction.

A new day is a chance for you to start over fresh if the day before didn't go as planned.

Your body is regenerating all the time.

Why are you putting the same old thought

patterns in a newly generated body?

Renew your mind like your body renews itself.

Rid yourself of jealousy, depression, failures,

lack of confidence and anxiety.

Tell yourself this is the day you shift the

negative to positive.

You are the creator of your own failures.

Negative beliefs give energy to the Universe to

bring your

failures to the physical realm.

So, stop holding on to your past.

Let go, think positive.

Have a burning desire for what you want in life.

Feel it like you already have it and your journey

will begin.

No one can make you happy.

Happiness comes from within.

It's up to you to bring it out.

So, get your Happy on.

Listen to your favorite song, get up and dance,

watch a funny show or movie.

Live and be grateful in the moment.

Sometimes it's not what you say to people.

It's how you say it.

Deliver it with a bit of compassion and maybe they

will receive it.

The Universe treats you how you treat yourself.

So, think good thoughts about how you feel about

yourself.

You will attract everything it has for you.

Life is like a garden.

Cultivate what you want.

You have to plant the seeds.

Have faith and believe in your desires.

Be intentional and watch your life blossom and

bear the fruit.

Don't get confused over choosing a religion.

God is always here with or without religion.

Spirituality puts you in a place where you can

love everyone and not have to argue about

religion.

We are all one mind here to live and evolve

knowing that God just wants us to love one

another.

Just because something went wrong during the day

shouldn't make your entire day bad.

You had a moment.

That's all it was, so keep looking forward and

move on.

Life is like driving.

There are signs to navigate you to your

destination.

You have to steer the wheel.

If you were concerned about your inside like you

are your outside,

You would have found your purpose by now,

Focus on your mind and we will see all of the

beauty that you behold,

Just like the leaves have a time to fall,

God sends you messages or signs to fall back from

things.

If you dismiss it, struggles will happen because

you can't change what was meant to die.

When you live in the spirit you don't have to

figure what's going to happen.

You go about your day and allow the Universe to

work.

Let your ego fall back for your true self to

precede you.

You will begin to feel the attraction of positive

energy from the Universe.

The energy will allow you to give the love that

is needed for humanity.

It doesn't matter what religion you are.

The message is always the same.

Love one another.

Let's stop separating ourselves because of religion

come together because of our spirituality.

Don't attach yourself to things.

They are here for you to enjoy, not become a

part of them.

You have disease filling on the inside from anxiety

and depression.

Your body is uneasy of the direction that you are

going.

Find your purpose and your body will go from

disease to at ease.

Time spent talking about the past is wasted

energy.

It serves you no purpose.

Having success in life doesn't mean that you are

on a level of higher conscious.

It simply means that you know how to make

money.

Thinking on a higher conscious makes you look

within to see how you can serve the Universe.

Everyone is trying to emulate everyone else.

The most powerful thing about you is "you".

God made only one of you stamped with your own

imprint.

So, bring out your own power.

You'll earn the stamp of approval from the most

important being, God.

Jump start your brain and give it a new network.

Do or learn something new.

Each time you have a new experience your brain

will start to rewire its neural connection.

So, let's start firing up those wires.

If your ego precedes you, you are blocking the

Universe from working through you.

When you use I, me and mine all of the time the

Universe doesn't have you.

Because you got "you".

How is that working for you?

One person can't change the world.

But if we all start having the thought process of

healing the world,

We can change it together.

The world is alive making all of your senses come to life.

The air is the breath of God and the rain is his purity washing over us.

Appreciate it and bask in every experience that nature gives you.

You have to continuously remind yourself that

there is a process in everything you do.

When hard times strike, continue to flow and

trust the process is already in effect.

When you are on a journey of evolving and people

around you are not.

Distance yourself from them.

While you are growing, their refusal to grow will

stunt yours.

Stop watching people live out their lives on

television.

Get out and have your own experiences.

It's not their real life anyway.

It's their "reality of life".

Taking baby steps in life will allow you to be

aware of every moment.

Being in the moment will allow you to make the

right choices in life to have a full and balanced

life.

The world says the best thing you can have is an education.

What good is it if you're not going to use it like God wanted.

He wants you to share your knowledge, not hold onto it and look down on others only to shame them for their lack of knowledge.

Toxic people can drain your energy.

Stop filling up your positive energy only to go

around negative people and let them use it up.

Envy and jealousy are poisons that seep into the

mind to make you feel less than.

Focus on yourself and not others and bring more

positive in your life.

You're too busy looking for the answers on the
outside.

When all you need is on the inside of you.

True happiness is having everything you need with nothing around.

The world is programming your thoughts to make

you think stuff will make you happy.

Program your own thoughts so that you can find

true happiness.

It will never be in things.

The destruction that is pouring out into the world

is coming from the minds of people.

Let's heal our minds and we will heal the world.

Everything has a process.

When you have a problem, don't fret.

The Universe is going through the process of

delivering you a solution.

Setting your mind on your intentions increases the

chance of you actually doing them.

So, get up with a mind of daily intention to make

the most of your day.

Society make us look at life in a shallow way.

Let's dig deeper into our mental capacity to live in

a higher conscious.

The world is always evolving, and you should too.

You are unique for a reason.

God gave us all different skills and talents to

share to the world.

Something special was given to you, so use it.